Autumn Season

Adult Coloring Book

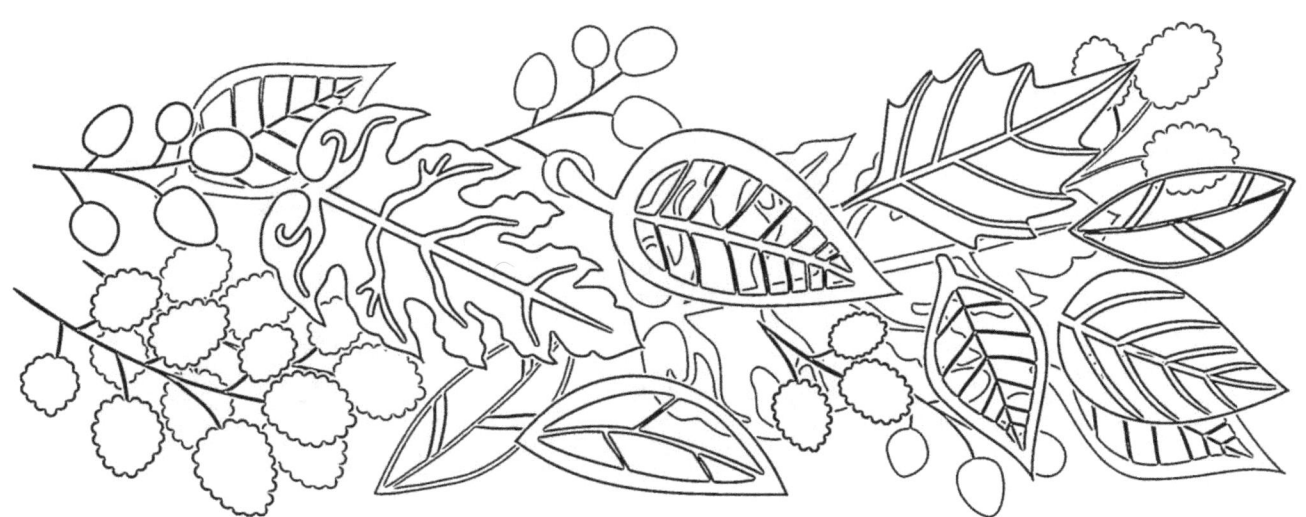

Copyright 2017 by Go and Color

All rights reserved. No part of this book may be reproduced in any form by any electronic or mechanical means including photocopying, recording, or information storage and retrieval without permission in writing from the publisher.

ISBN-13:978-1975988876

ISBN-10:1975988876

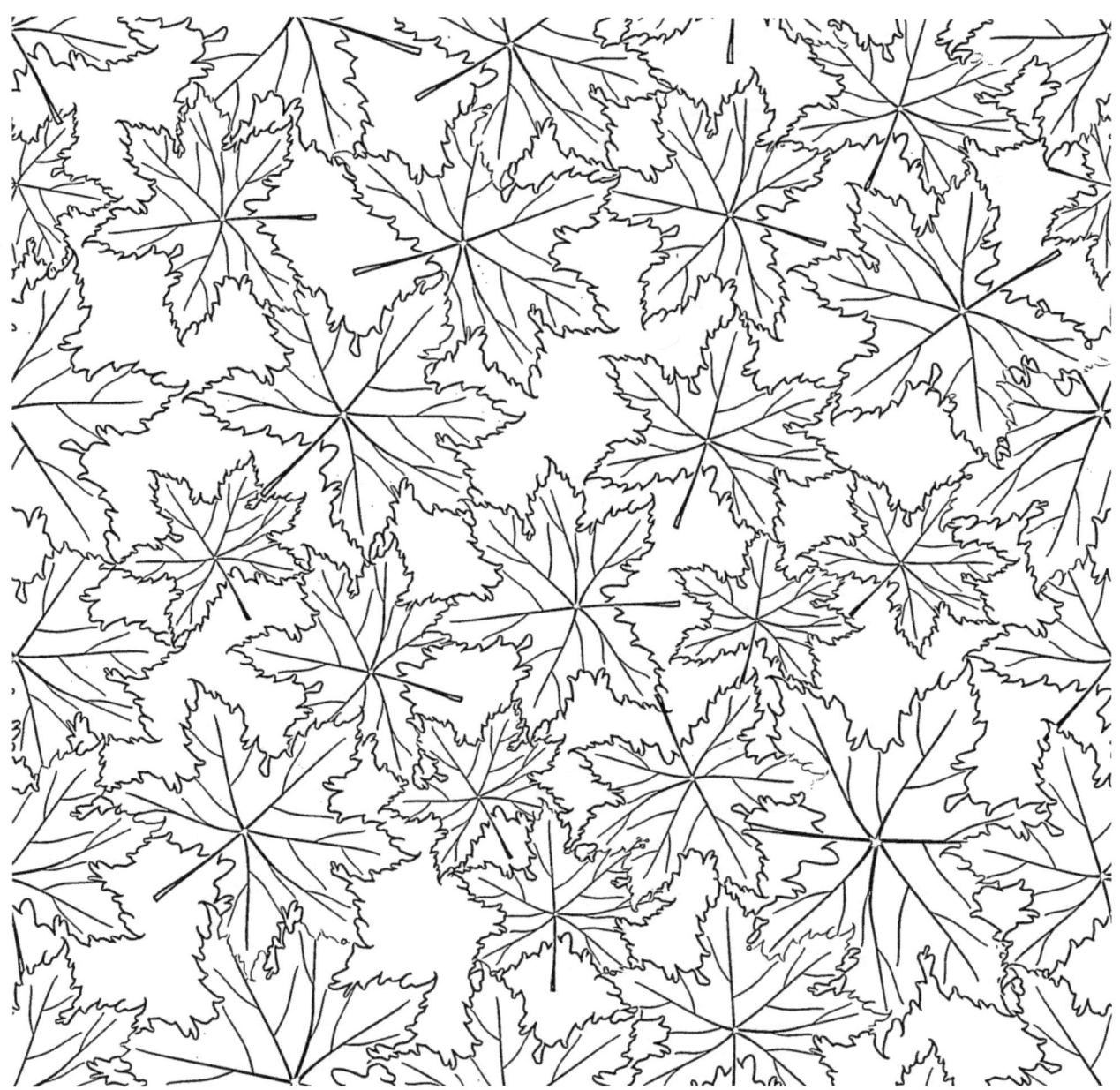

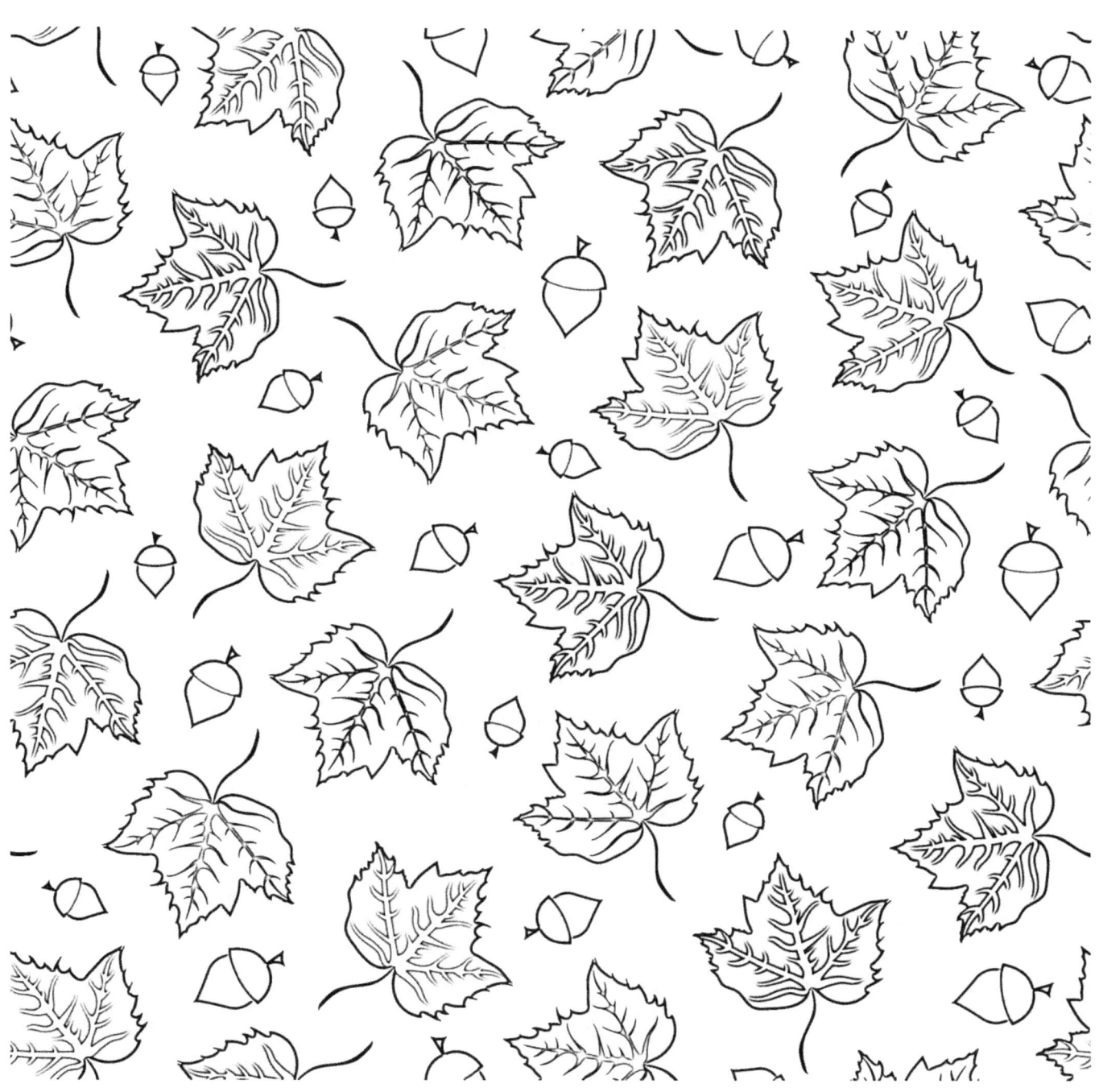

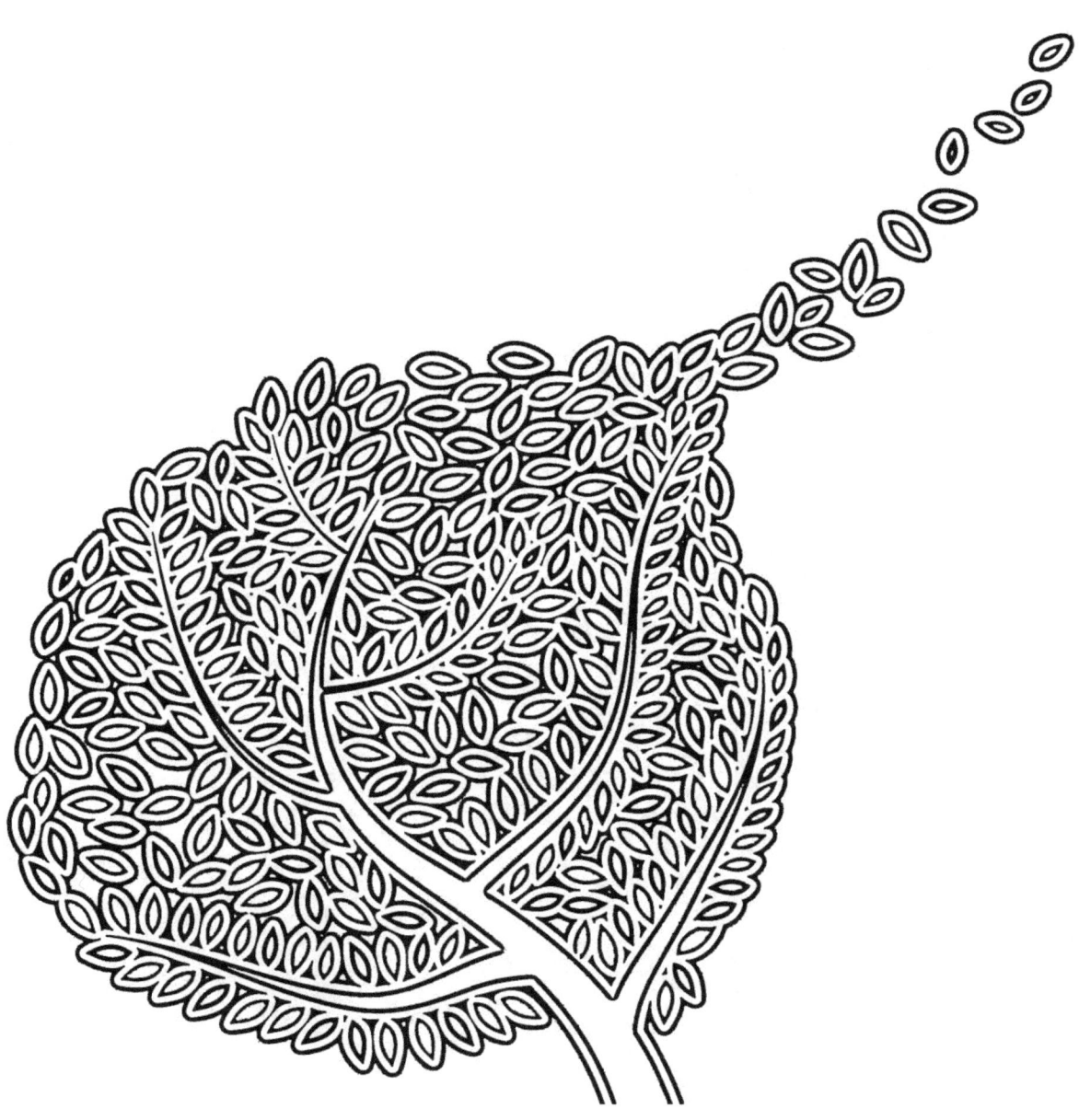

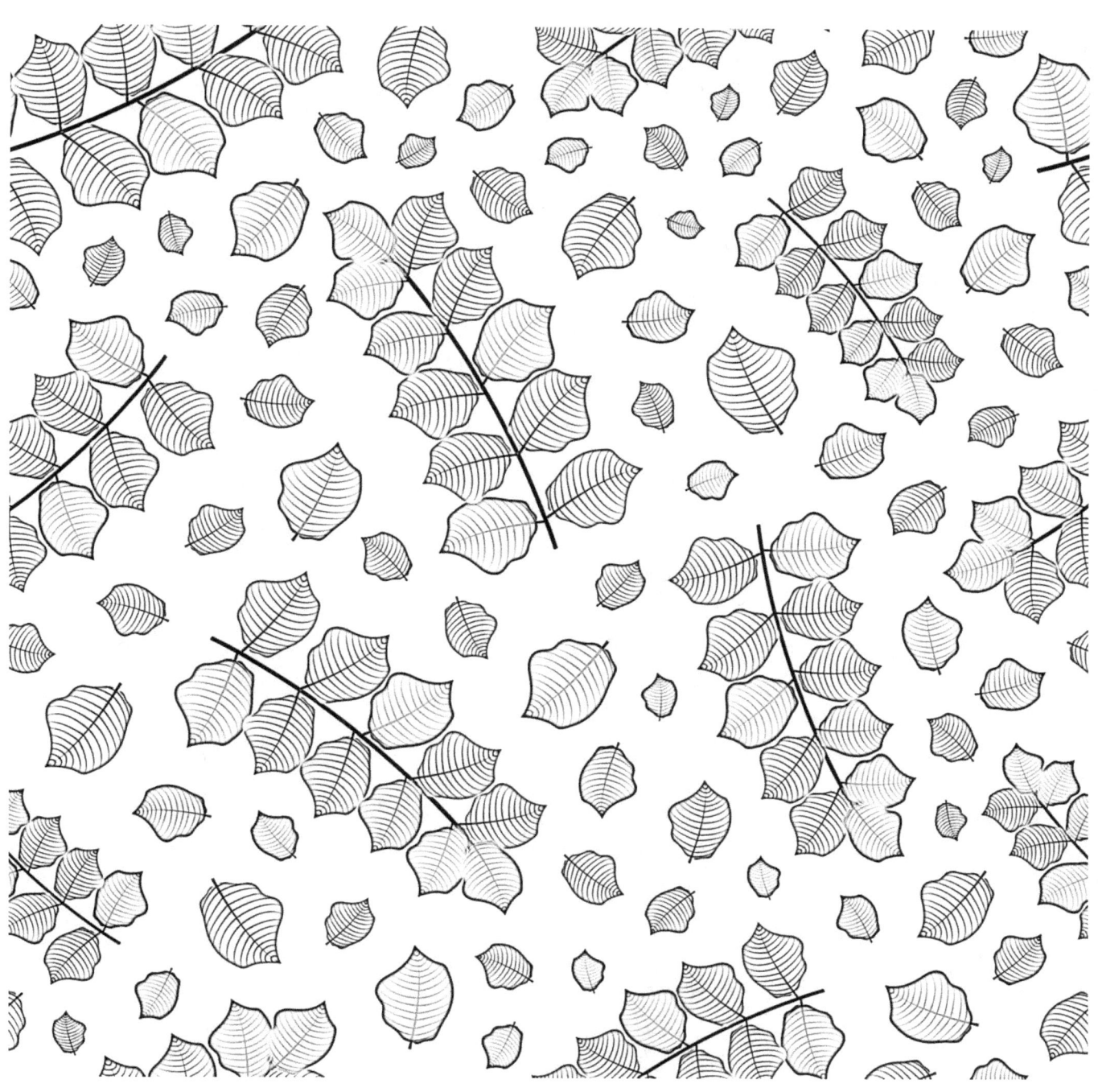

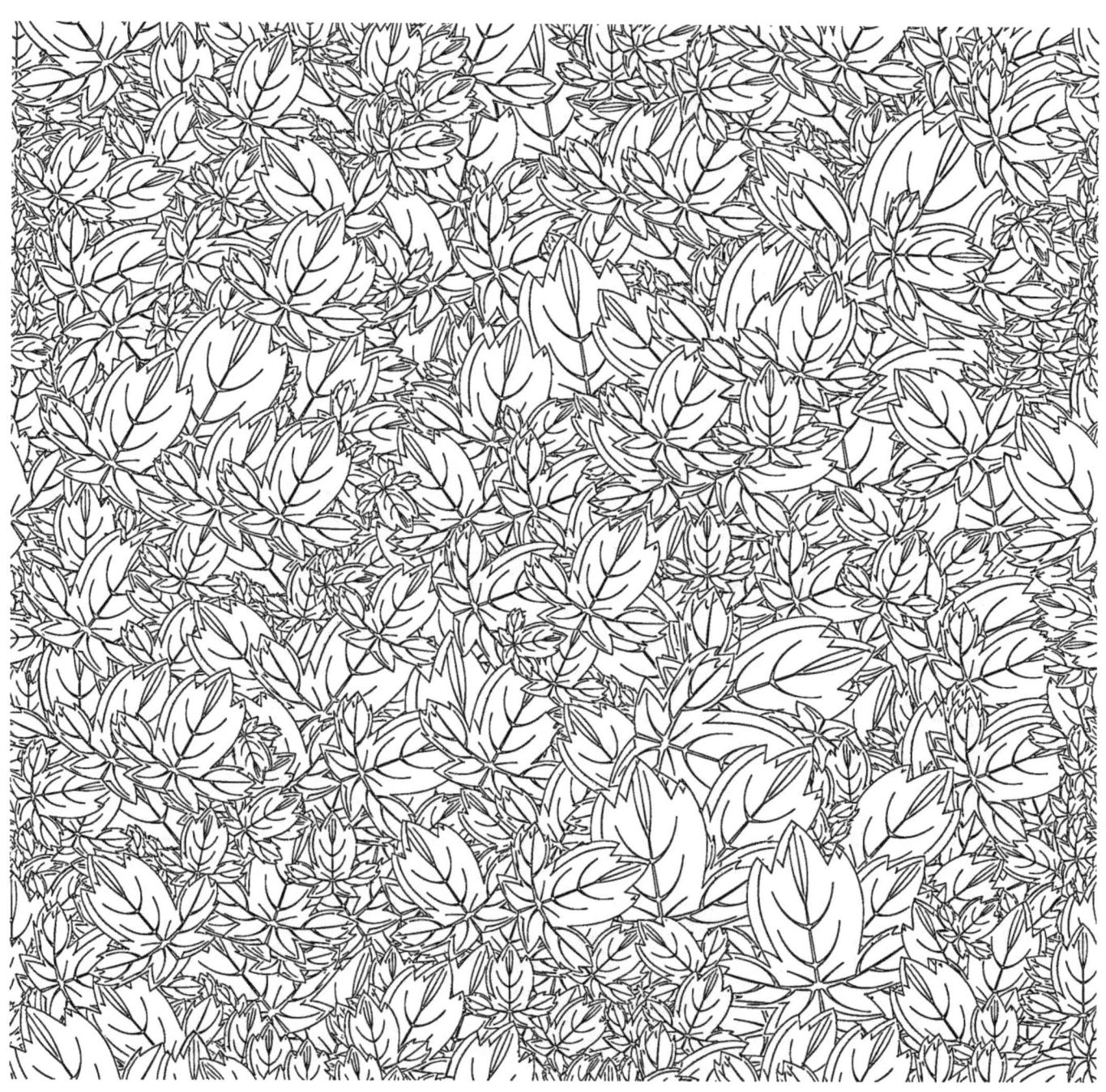

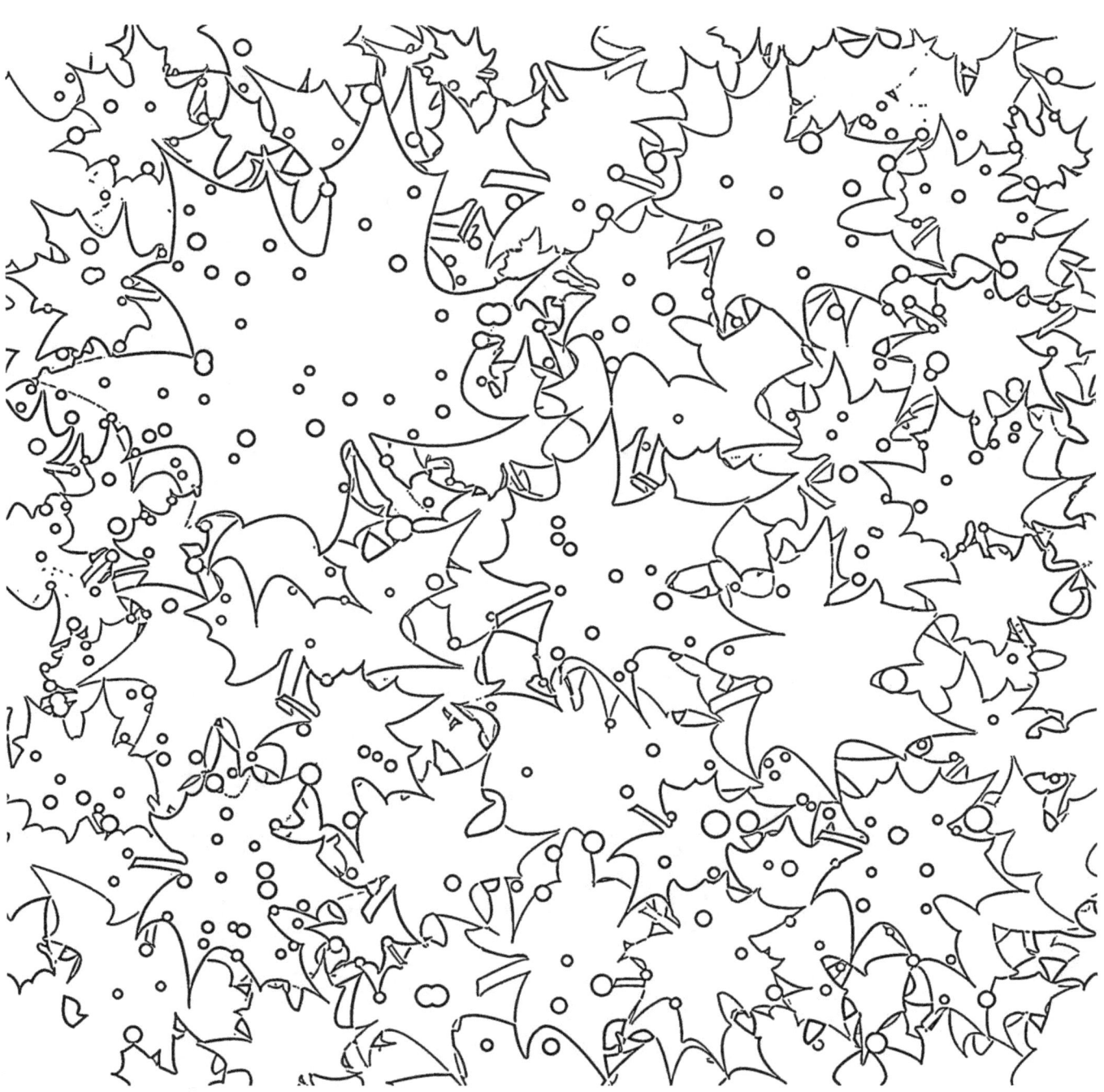

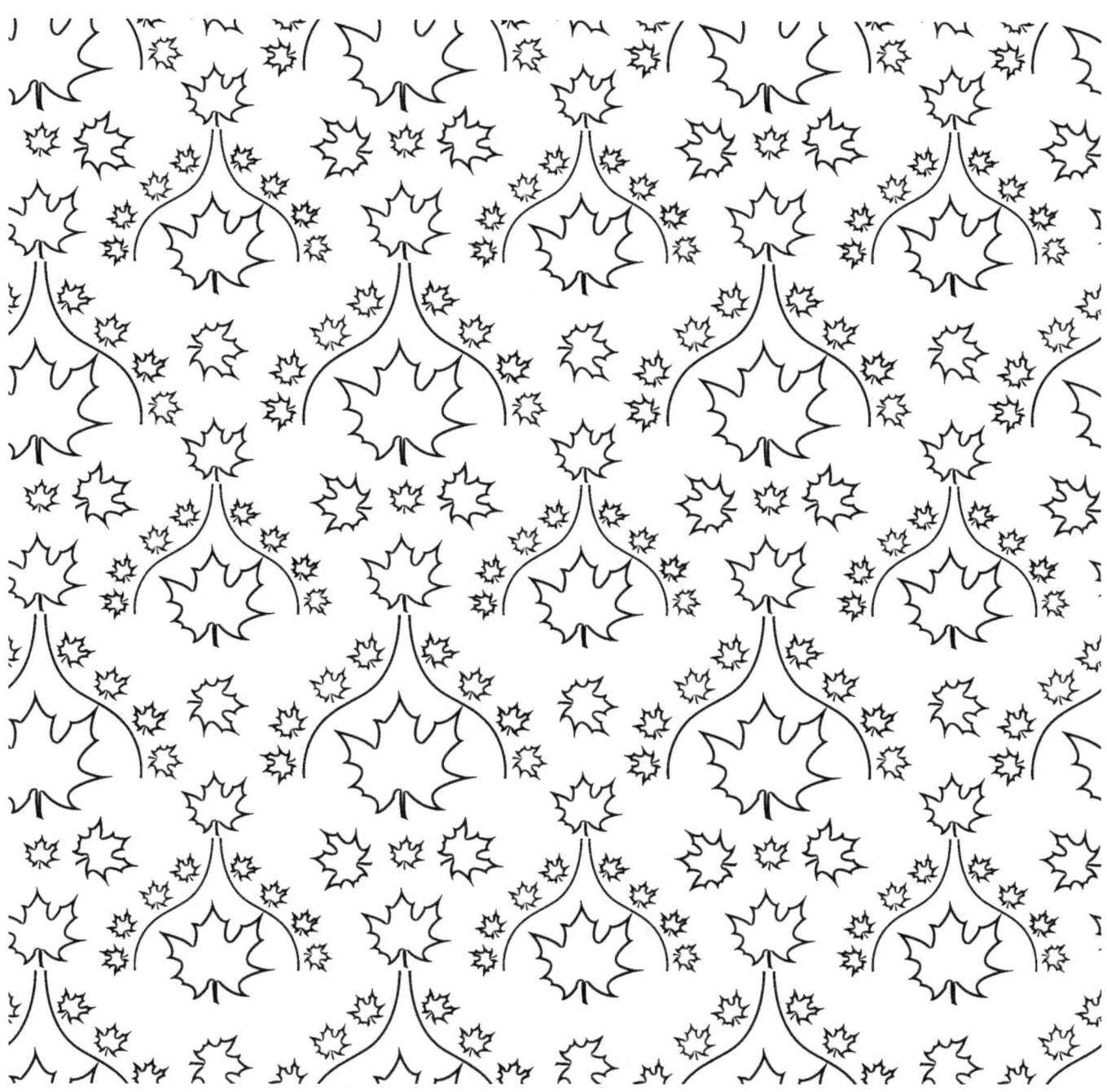

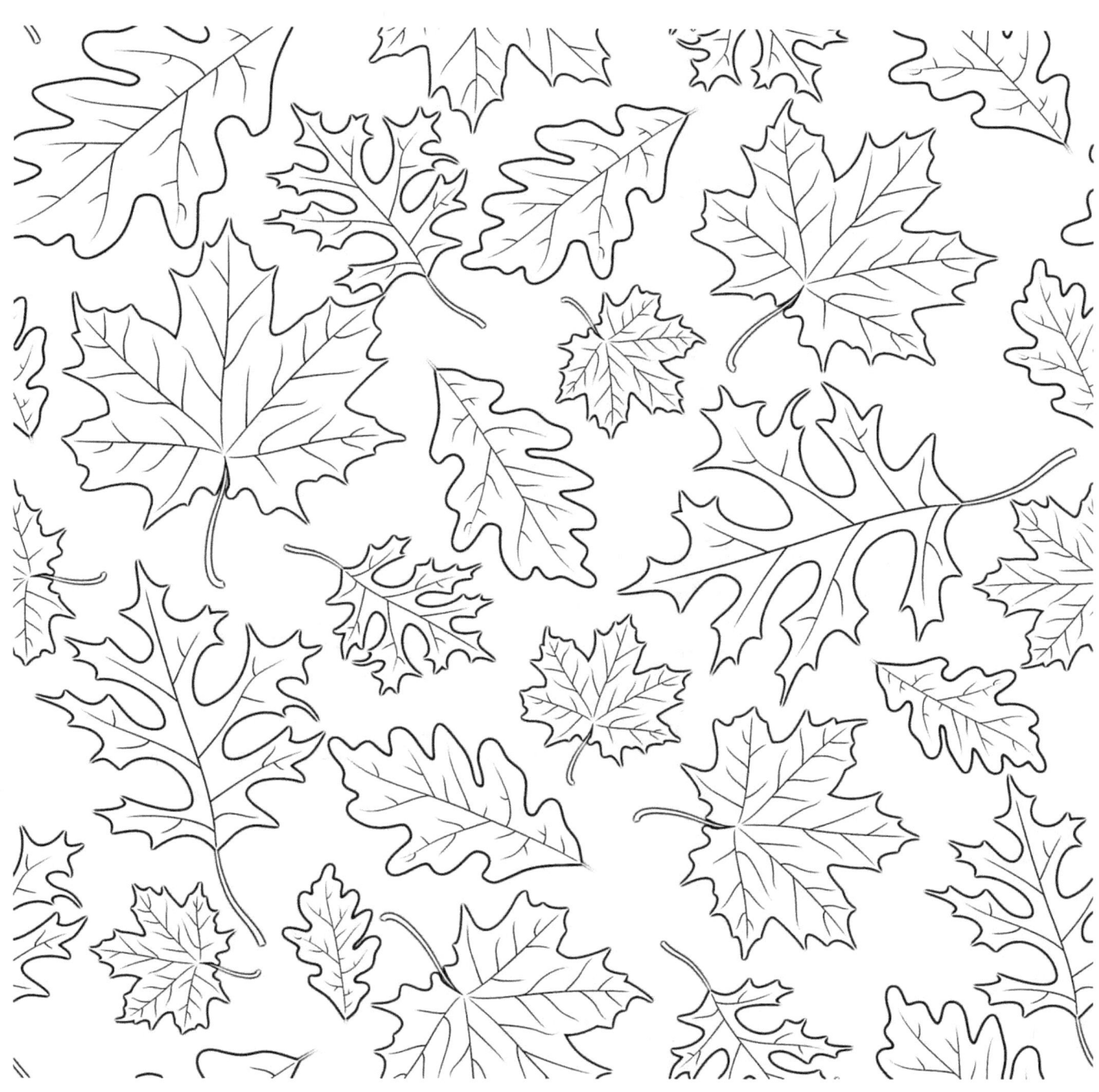

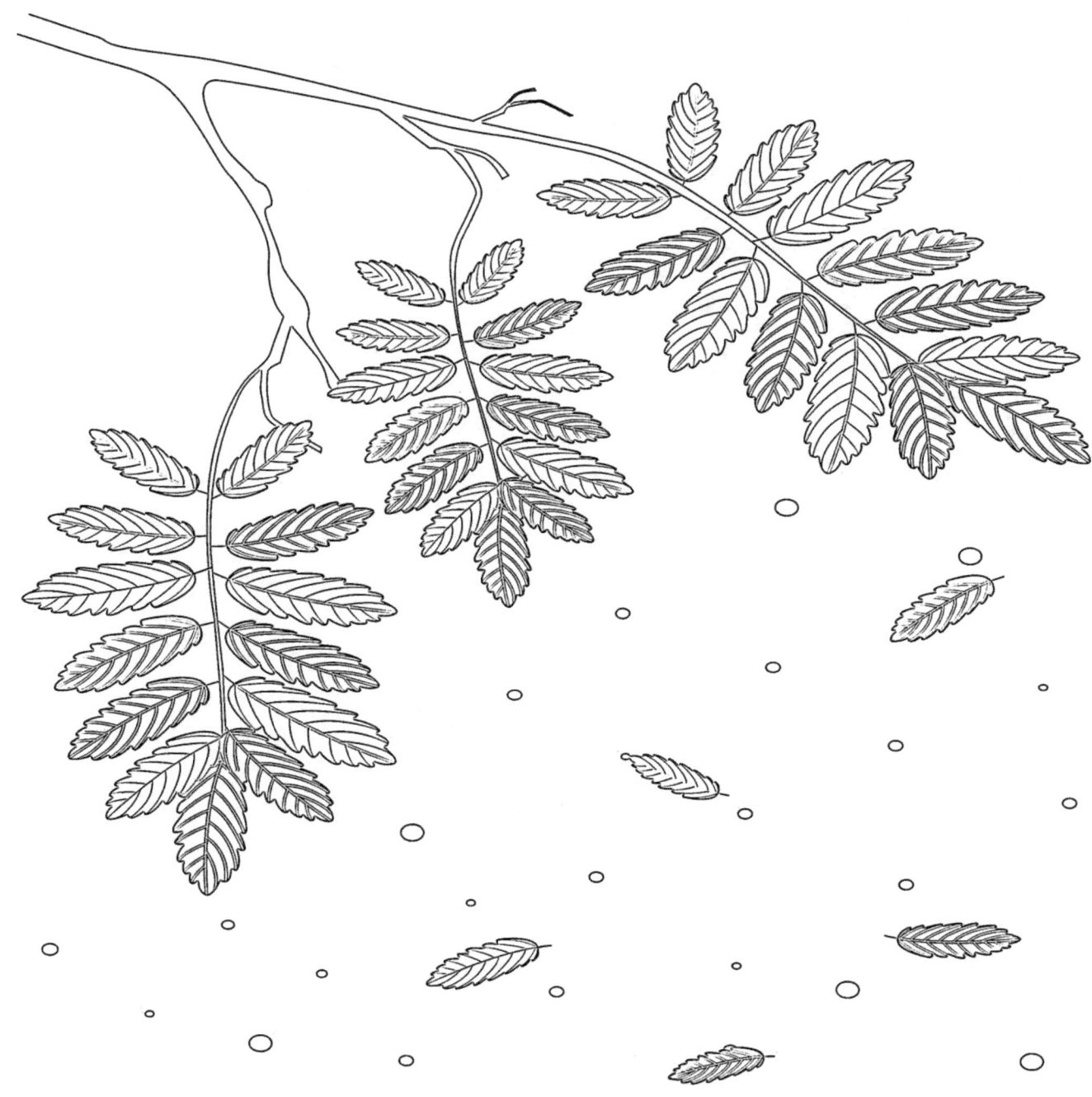

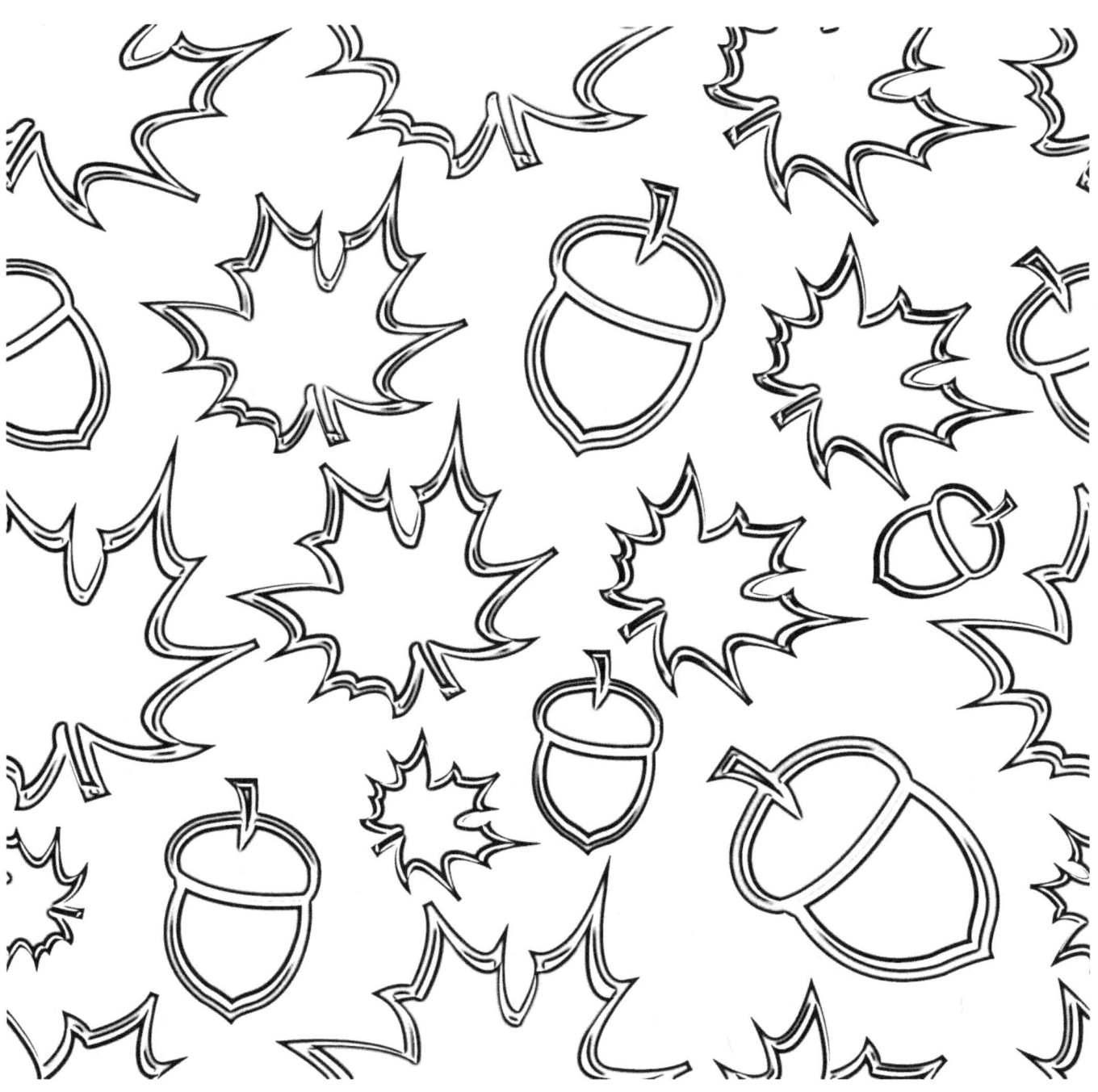

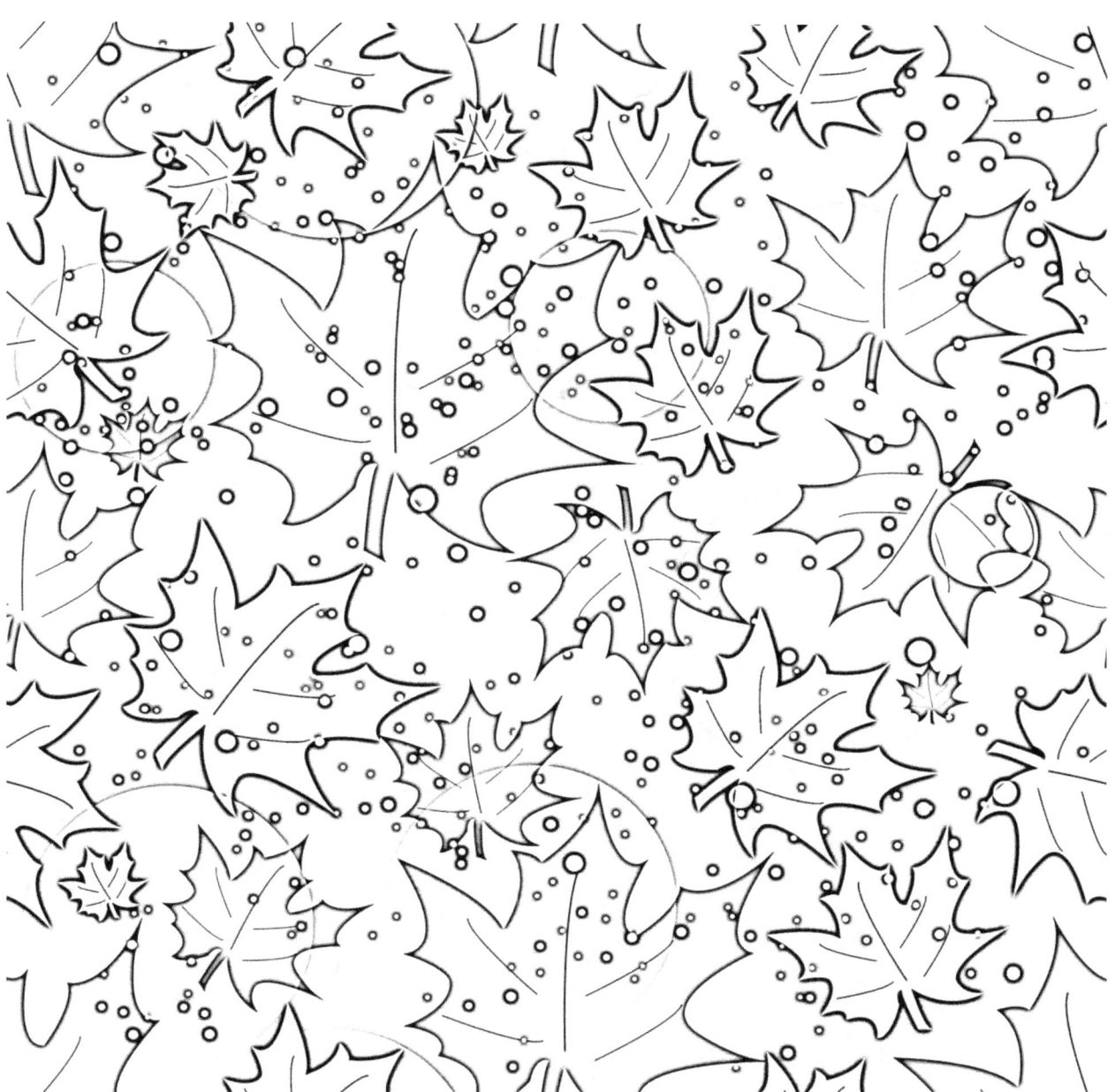

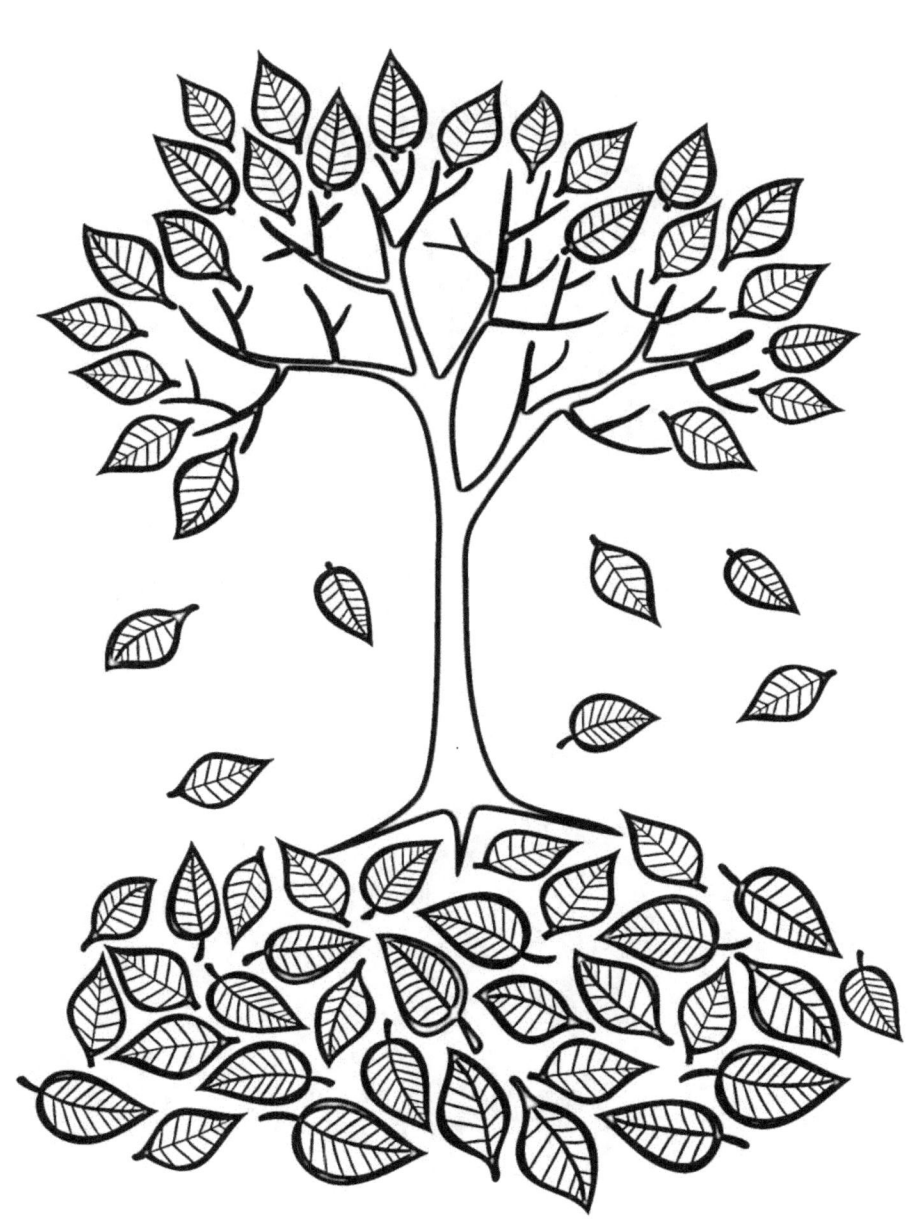

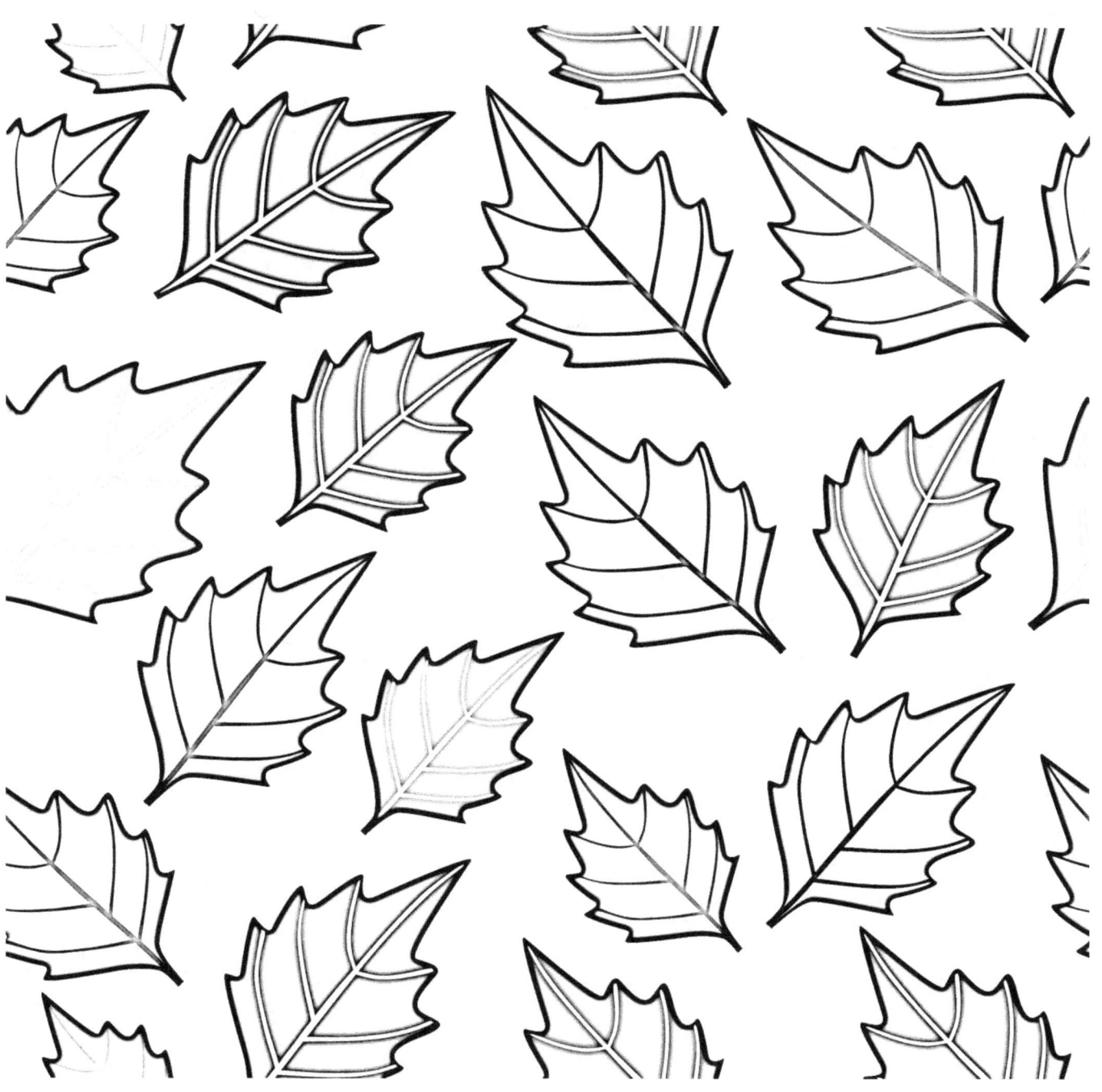

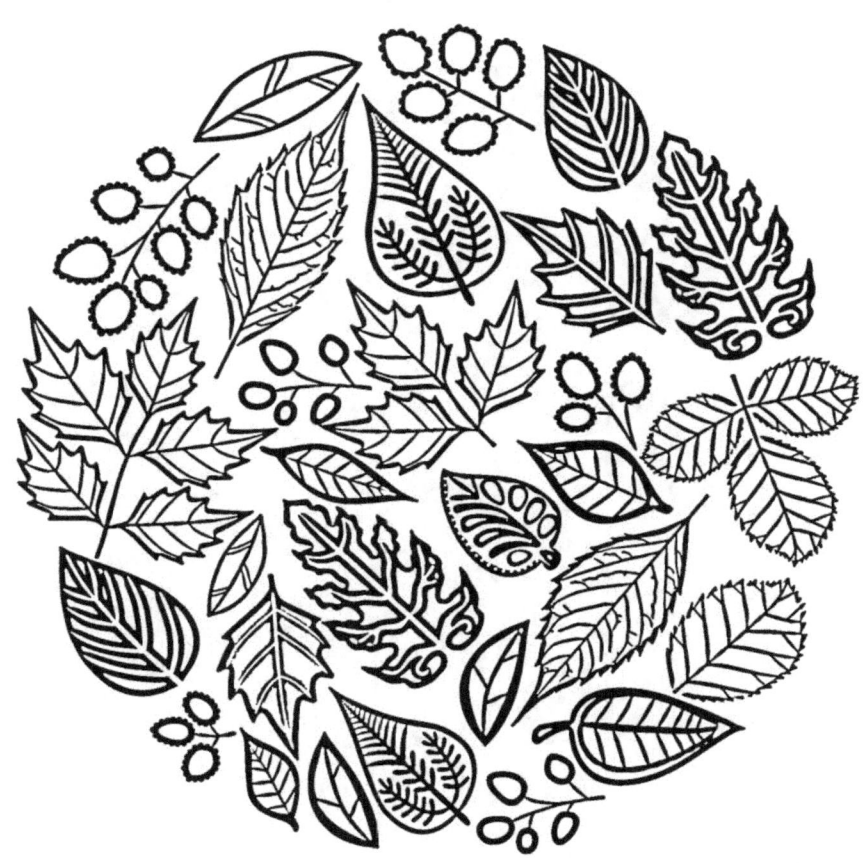

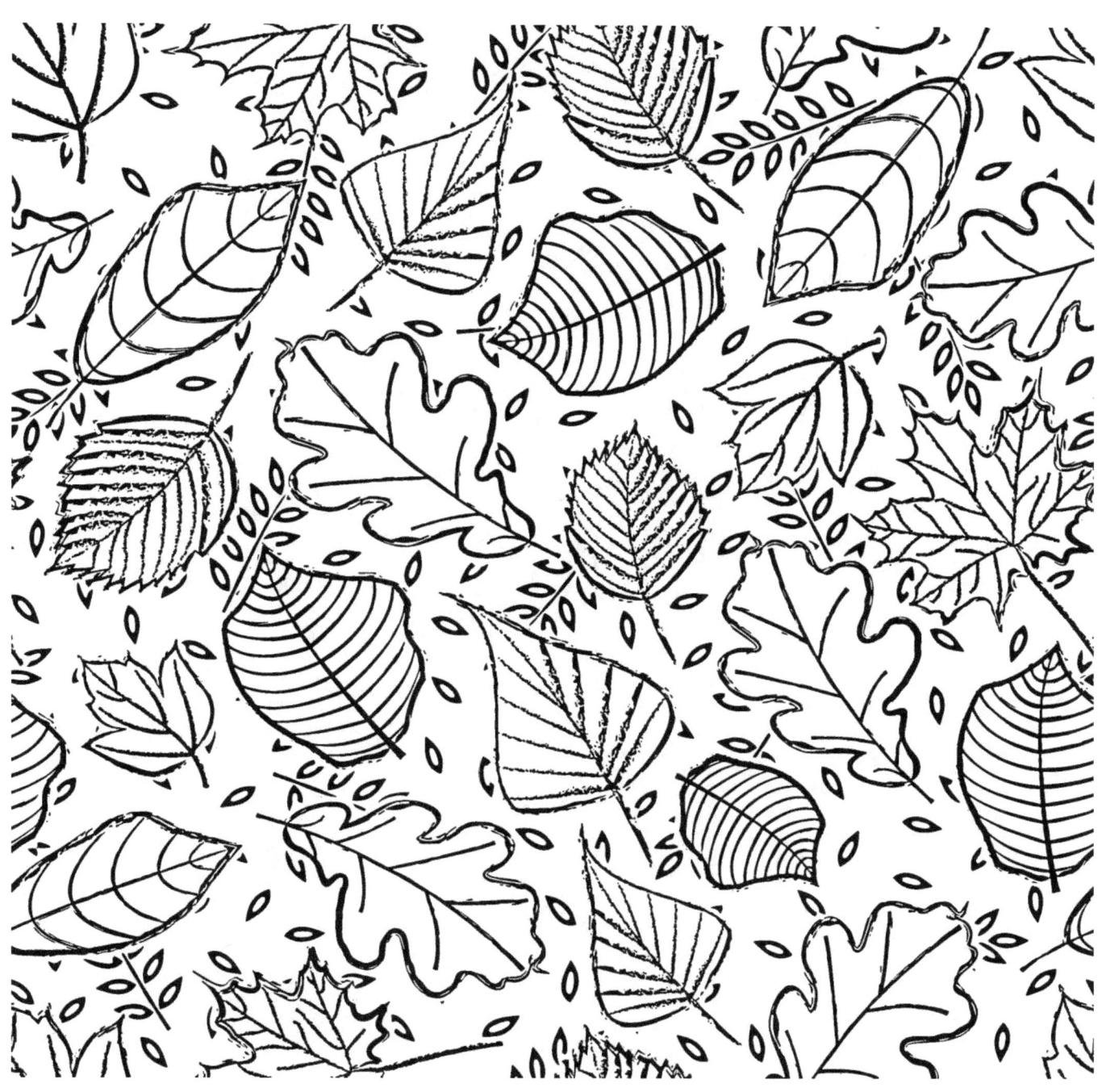

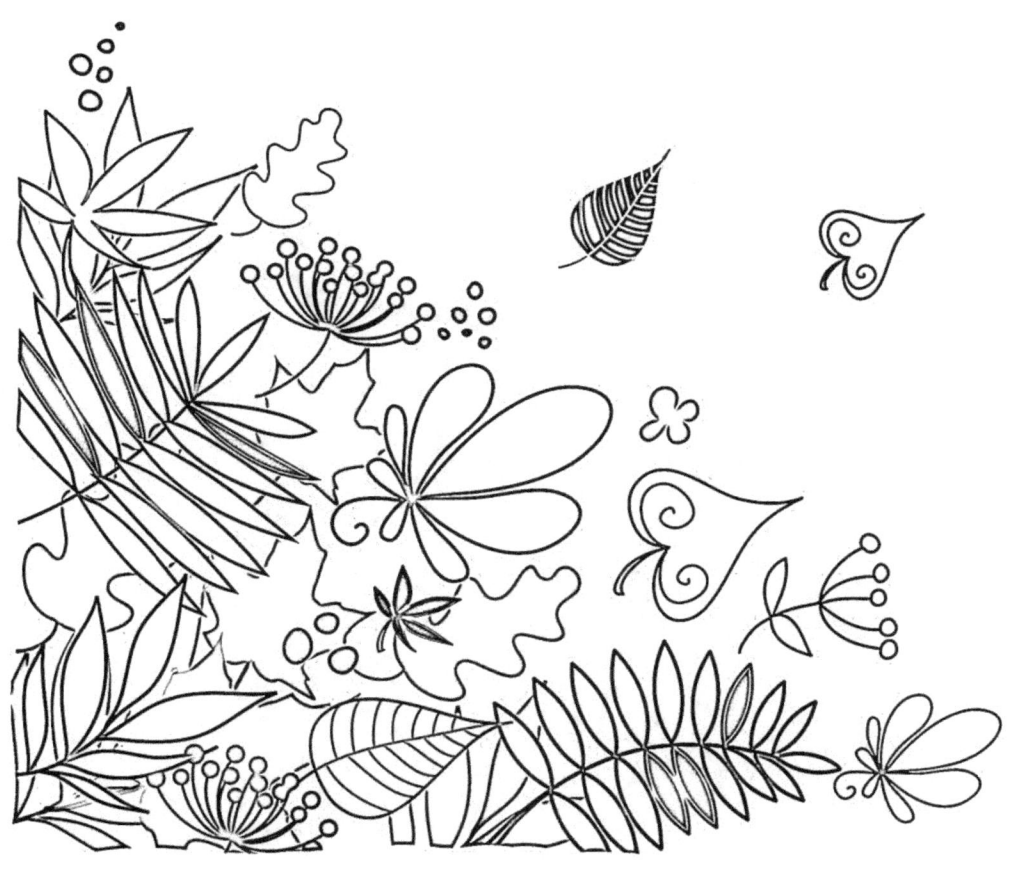

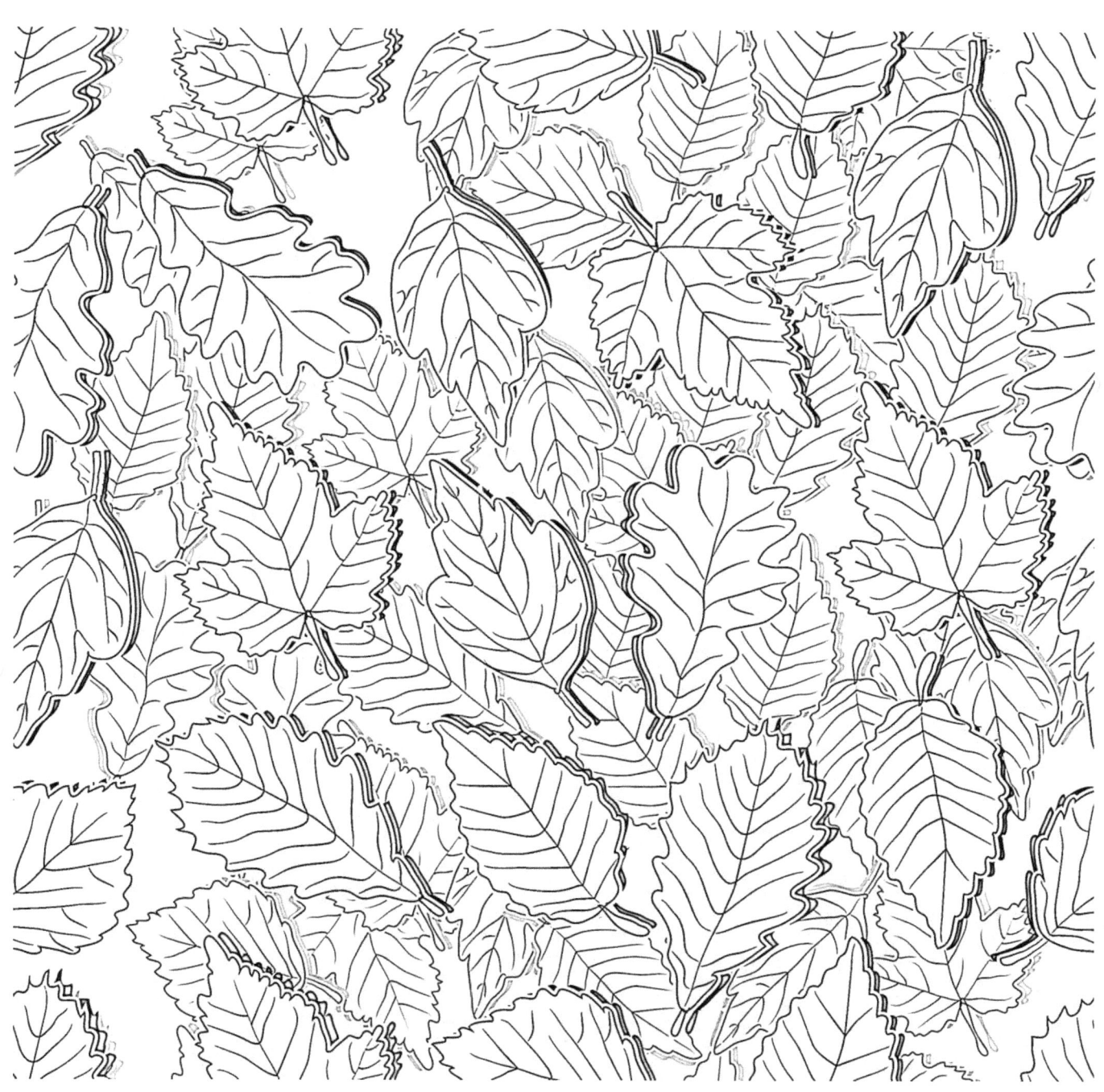

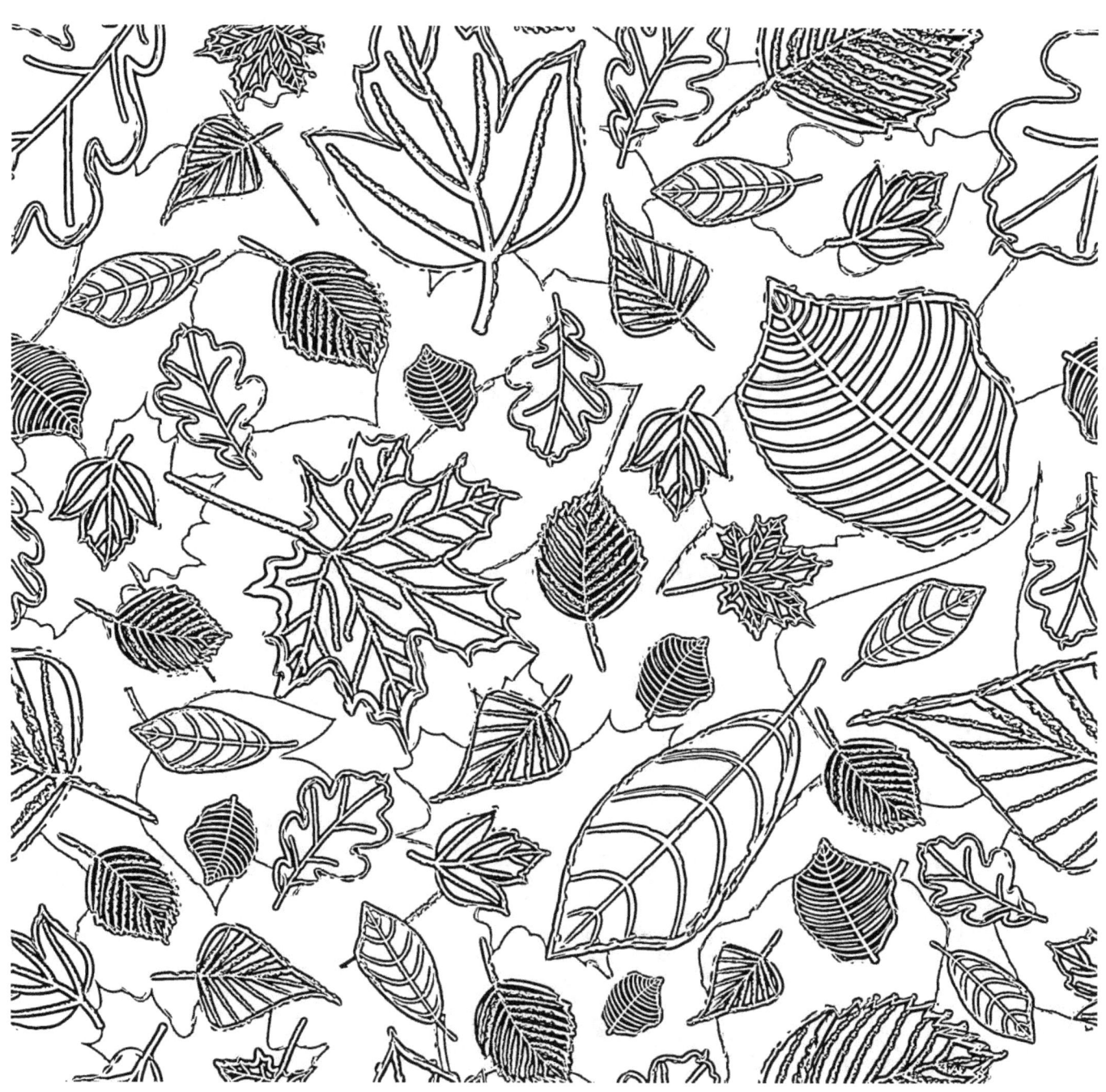

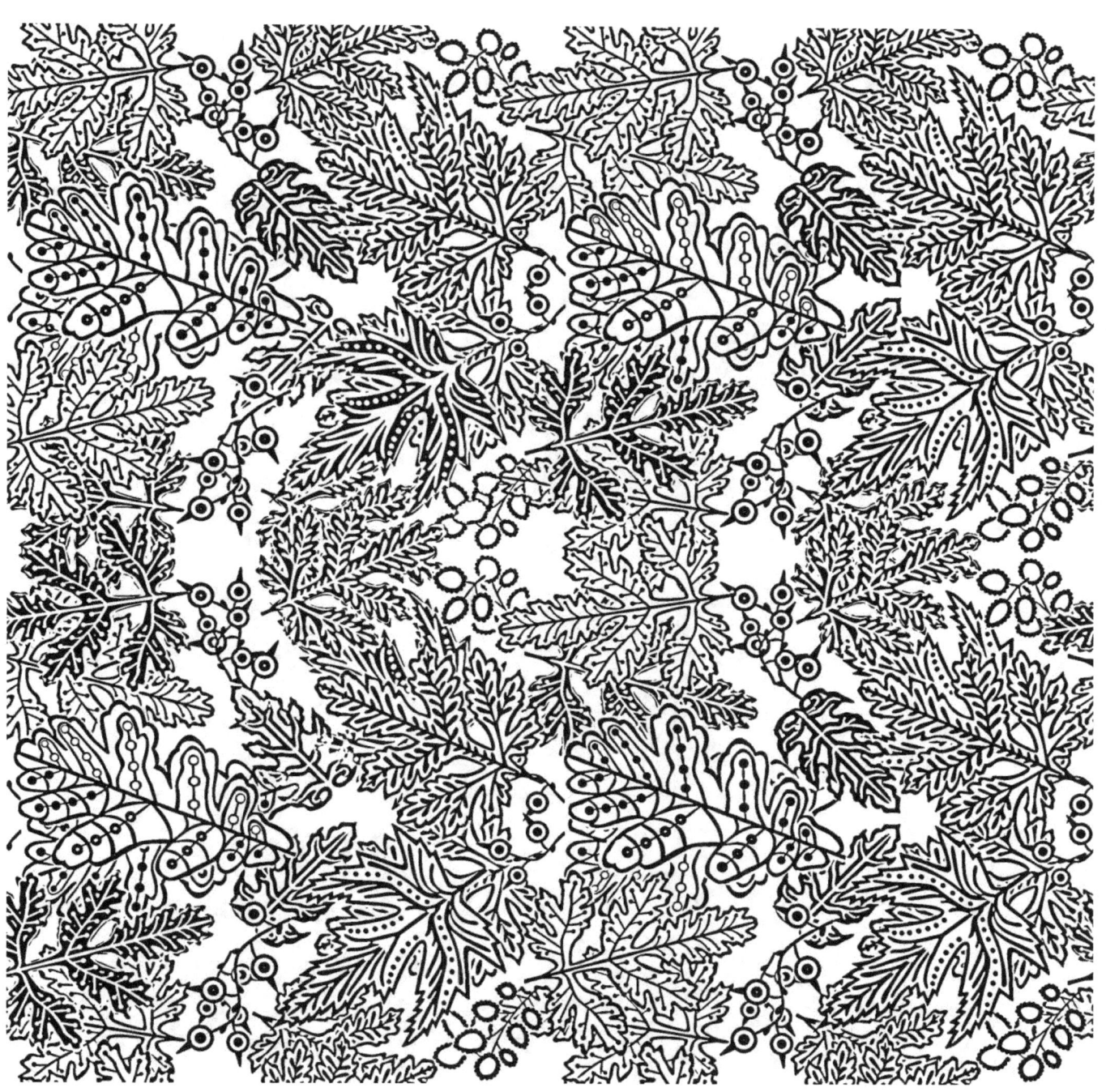

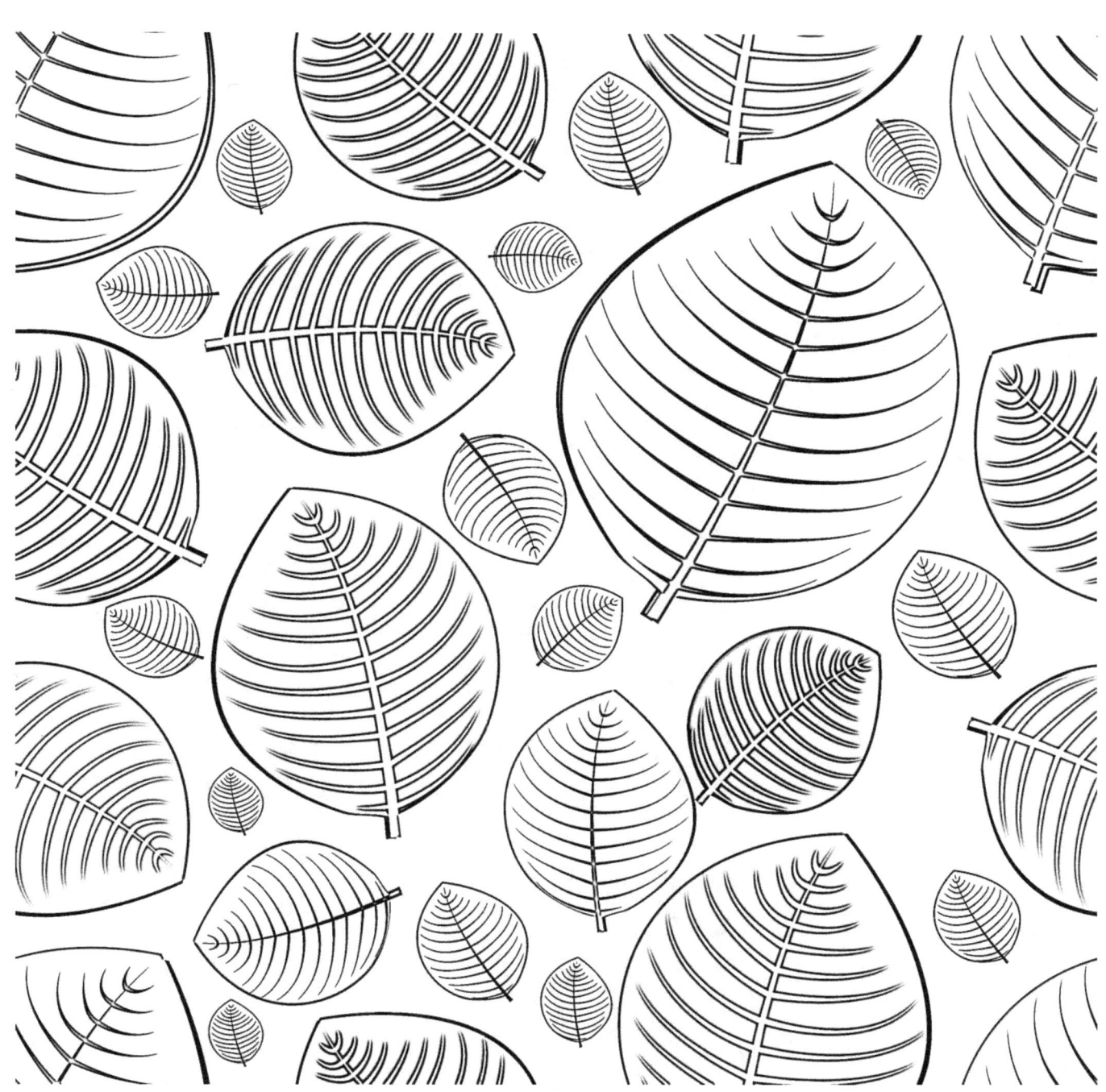

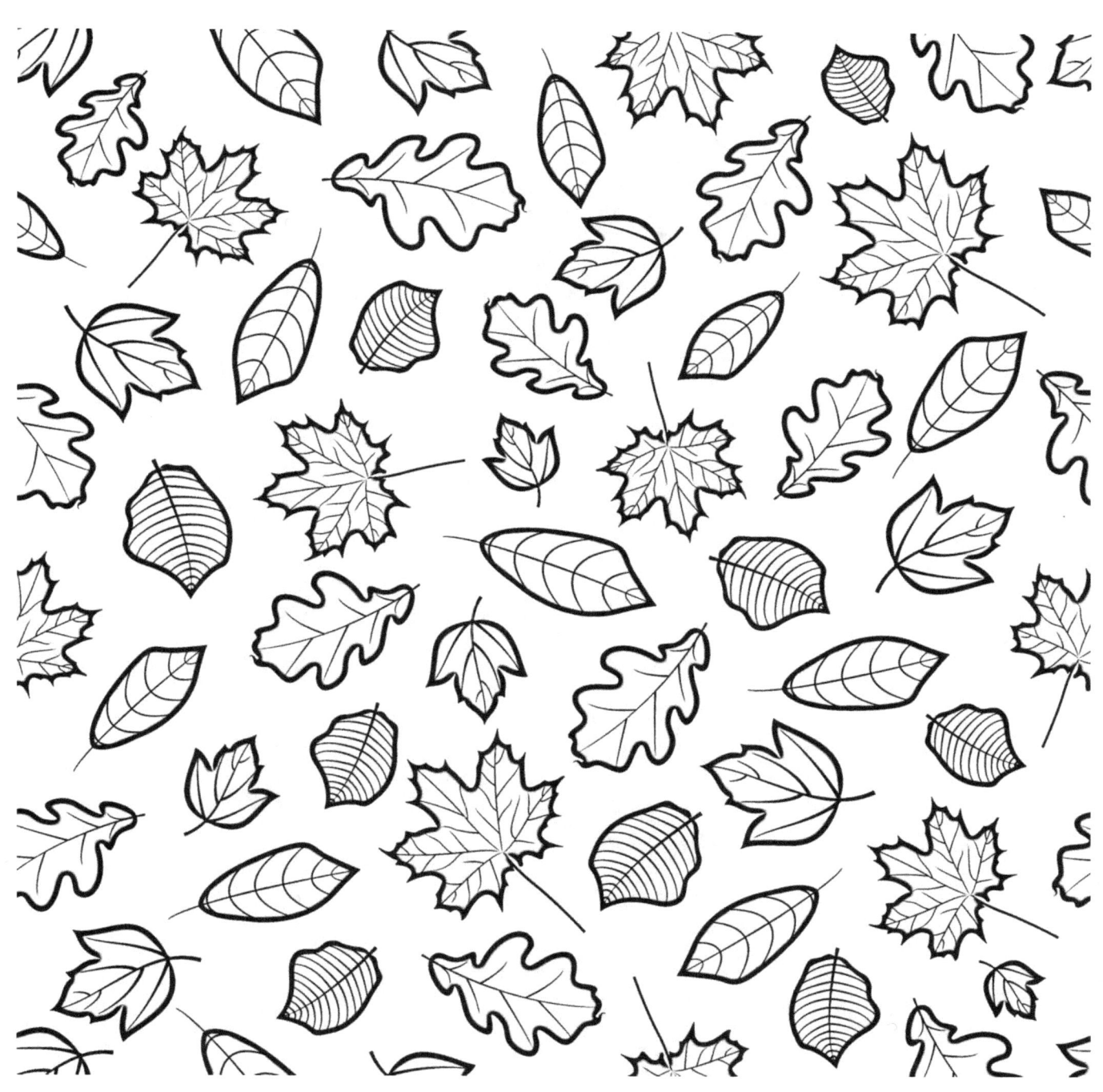

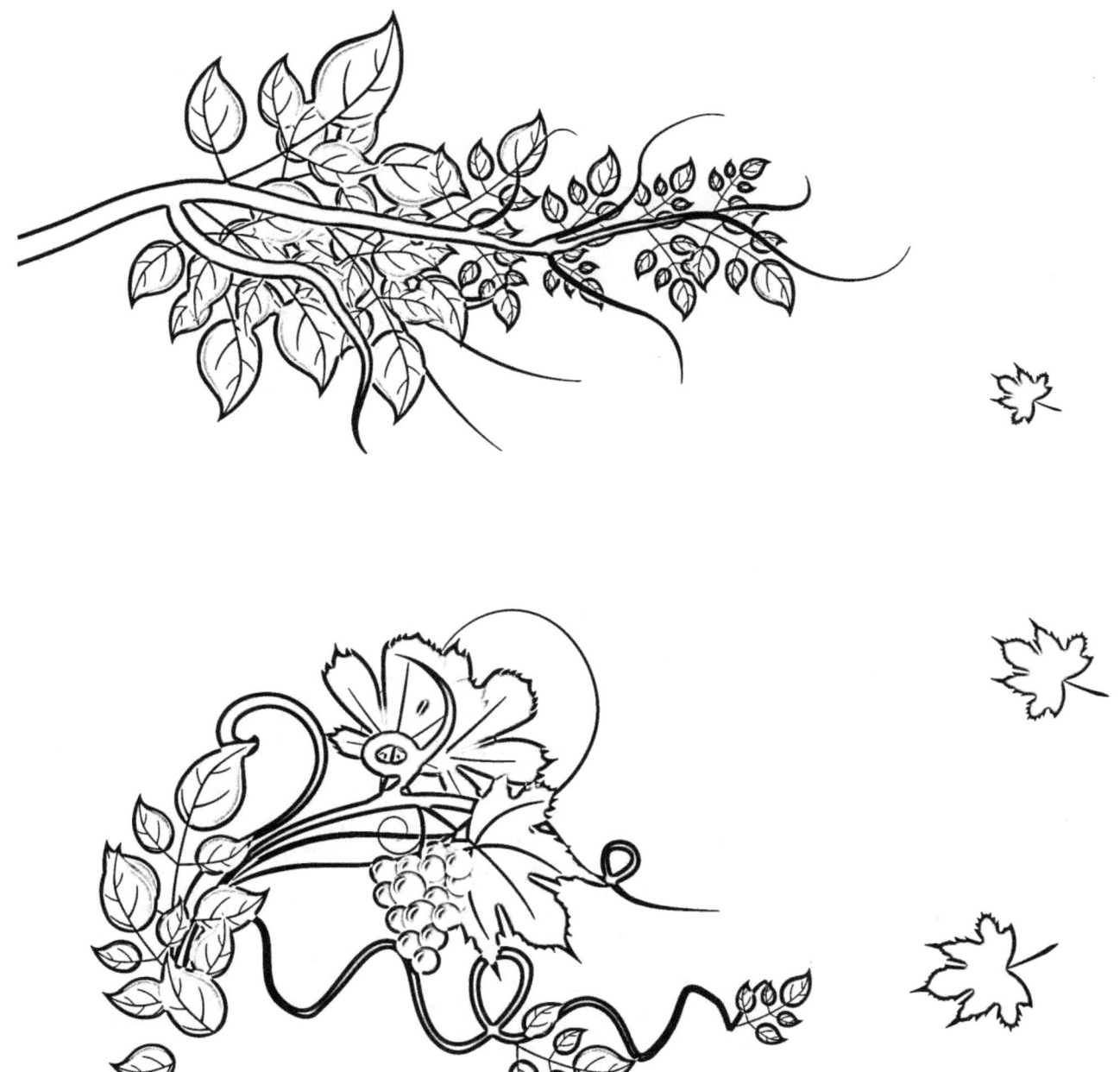

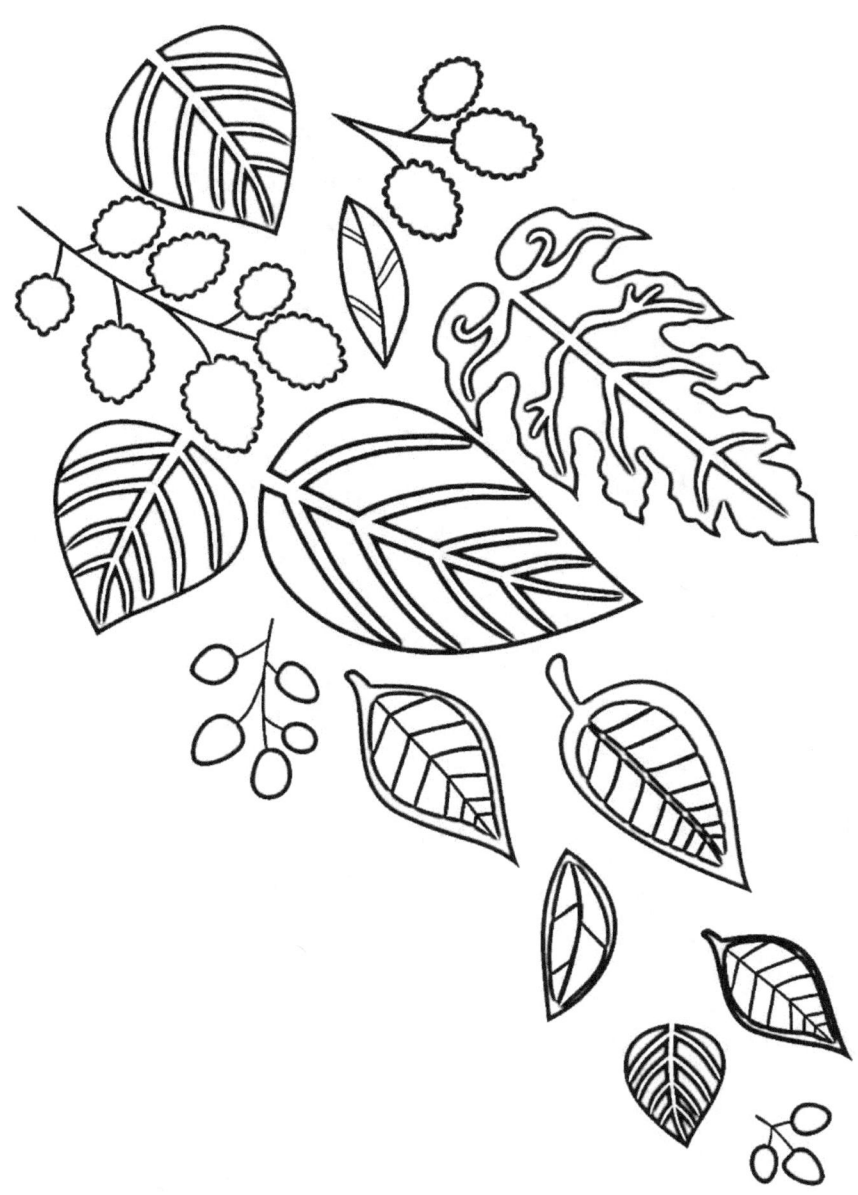

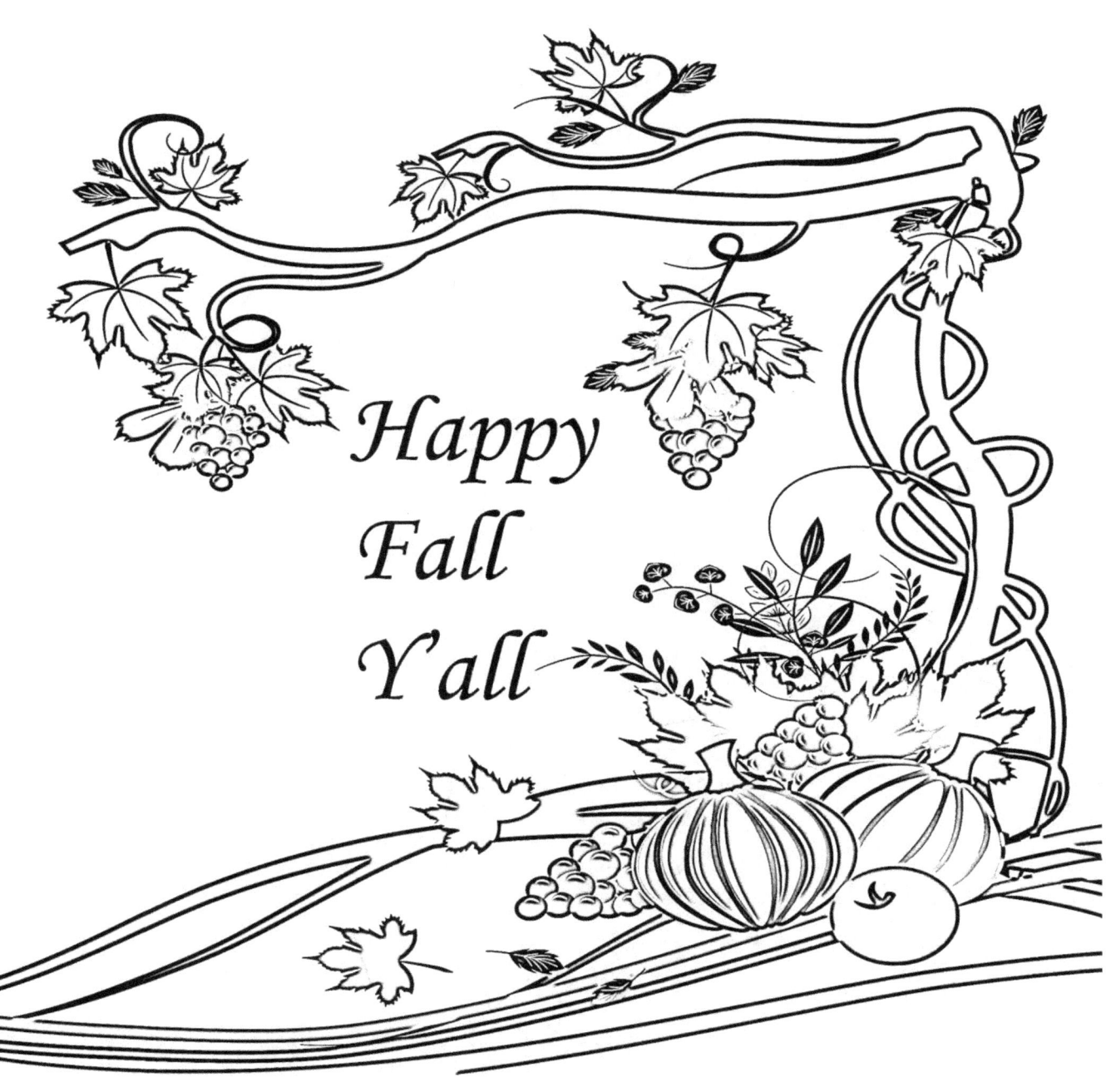